THE TRAP

To innocent children everywhere. —KHN

For Hannah and Nate, with love. —DB

Text © 2008 Karmel H. Newell
Illustrations © 2008 Dan Burr

Visit us at DeseretBook.com

Library of Congress Cataloging-in-Publication Data

Newell, Karmel H.
   The trap : a story to help teach children modesty and protect them from pornography / Karmel H. Newell.
      p.   cm.
   ISBN 978-1-59038-929-4 (hardbound : alk. paper)
   1. Pornography—Religious aspects—Christianity.   2. Pornography—Religious aspects—The Church of Jesus Christ of Latter-day Saints.   I. Title.
   BV4597.6.N49 2008
   241'.667—dc22   2008006614

Printed in Mexico
R. R. Donnelley and Sons, Reynosa, Mexico

10   9   8   7   6   5   4   3   2   1

THE TRAP

A STORY TO HELP TEACH CHILDREN MODESTY AND PROTECT THEM FROM PORNOGRAPHY

WRITTEN BY

Karmel H. Newell

ILLUSTRATED BY

Dan Burr

DESERET
BOOK

Salt Lake City, Utah

Jason couldn't wait any longer. His stomach was tight, and his hands were sweaty. He inched his way around the corner of the house to where his dad was lifting the wasp trap off its hook.

"Jason, look at this," his dad marveled. "Can you believe these yellow jackets?"

Jason tried to act interested. "Yeah, so many of them."

"Why would they fly into the trap when their family and friends were already dead on the bottom?"

"The poison must have smelled really good to them," Jason said.

"I guess." His dad shook his head.

Jason's dad set down the trap and took off his gloves.
"Here, Jason, take a look for yourself."

But Jason didn't seem to hear him.

"Are you all right?" His dad stopped what he was doing and looked at him. "It's not like you to turn down a chance to get close to some bugs."

His dad smiled just enough to give Jason the courage to talk.

Dad, when I was at Matt's house today, we were on the Internet. I'm not sure what we typed—we must have made a mistake—but a picture popped up that was really bad. We couldn't get it off the screen. Now I can't seem to stop thinking about it." Two brave tears

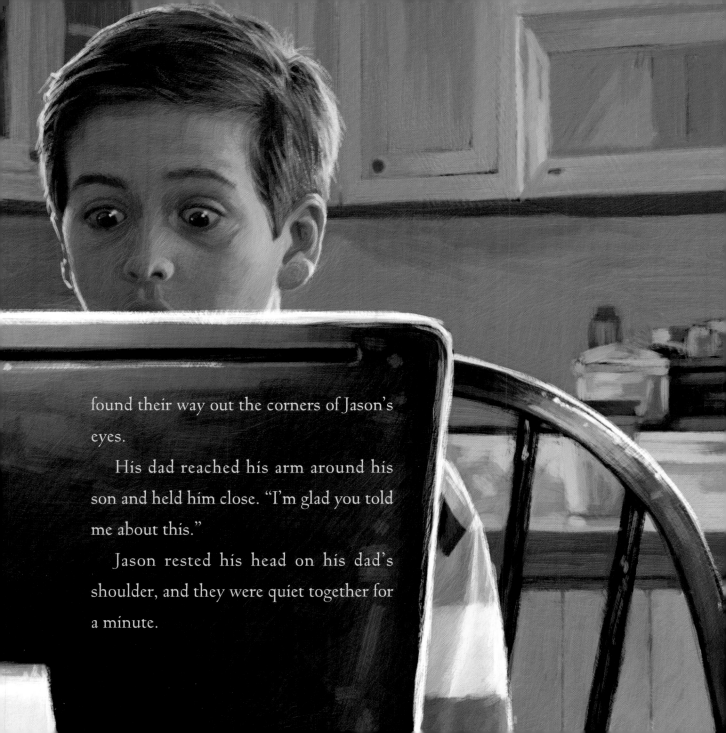

found their way out the corners of Jason's eyes.

His dad reached his arm around his son and held him close. "I'm glad you told me about this."

Jason rested his head on his dad's shoulder, and they were quiet together for a minute.

Jason, it sounds like what you saw today was pornography. I know you didn't mean to, and I can see you felt how evil it was. Most people aren't looking for it the first time they see it. But if they start looking for it, they can become more addicted to it than to drugs or alcohol. Just like these wasps, they can trap themselves—and their families—so they can't live and love like Heavenly Father wants them to."

Jason's dad explained, "When a yellow jacket is attacked, it sends out an alarm to its nest mates. What you felt today was a kind of alarm. The Holy Ghost was warning you so that you wouldn't get trapped, much like you warned your sister not to play by the apple tree after you got stung there."

Jason moved to a bench on the patio. His dad leaned forward and put his hand on Jason's knee.

"Maybe that's hard for you to understand. Let me try to explain it this way. Have you ever thought that our bodies make it possible for us to have families? Heavenly Father wants His spirit children to come to a mother and a father who will love them and keep them safe. Immodesty and pornography destroy families. They trap people into thinking about themselves more than they think about their families."

I'm getting ahead of myself, though . . . In the very beginning, after God made the world, hung the stars in the sky, planted all the seeds, and made every living creature on the land and in the sea, He created the first man and woman.

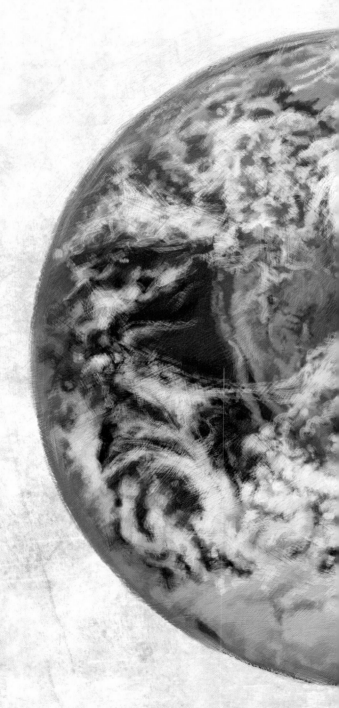

"They were His greatest creations. God called them Adam and Eve. They were the first spirits to come to earth and receive bodies. They were so happy. With their bodies, they could run and jump; they could touch and taste and smell as never before.

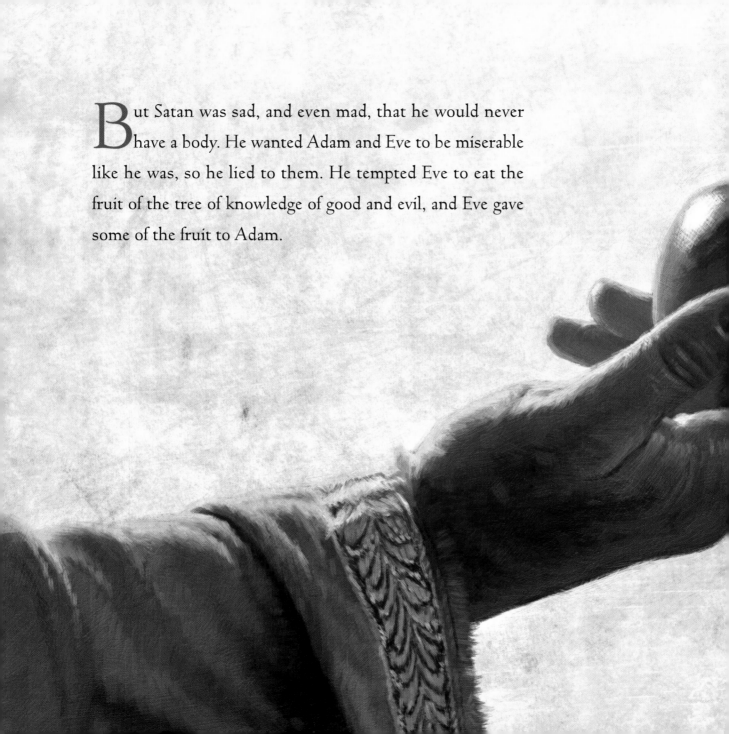

But Satan was sad, and even mad, that he would never have a body. He wanted Adam and Eve to be miserable like he was, so he lied to them. He tempted Eve to eat the fruit of the tree of knowledge of good and evil, and Eve gave some of the fruit to Adam.

"After they ate the fruit, for the first time they understood what it meant to be naked. Adam and Eve sewed fig leaves together to cover themselves, but when they heard the Lord's voice, they tried to hide."

Jason pulled a leaf off the maple tree by the patio and twirled it by the stem.

Satan may want us to feel like hiding, but Heavenly Father wants us to be happy and feel good about the choices we make. The Lord called Adam and Eve close to Him and taught them. Before Adam and Eve left the Garden of Eden, He made clothes for them out of animal skins. In other words, He taught them how to dress modestly. He knew we would feel bad—and even trap our spirits—if we showed off our bodies or if we started looking at other people who were showing off their bodies."

Jason's dad emptied the wasps into a sack and refilled the trap with more of the deadly attractant. A few drops spilled onto his hands, and he quickly washed them clean with the garden hose.

"Jason, Jesus Christ doesn't just help us to avoid traps. He leads us out of them. Like the water from the hose washing the poison from my hands, the power of Christ's Atonement can wash away the poison of bad thoughts and pictures.

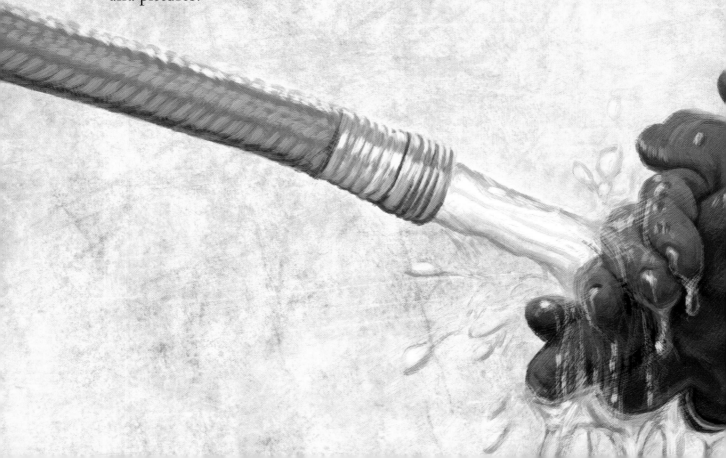

"Jason, what do you think you should do if you ever see pornography again?"

"Turn away from it. Turn off the computer, if that's where it is. And tell you or Mom."

That's right. Now, would you like to say a prayer with me? Let's ask Heavenly Father to help you forget what you saw. I know He can. By keeping your mind and body clean, someday you'll be able to go to the temple. The temple is a lot like the Garden of Eden. When you go there, you feel close to Heavenly Father and Jesus. You know that They love you, and you don't want to do anything that would keep you from feeling Their love again and again."

Jason smiled as he put on his dad's gloves and stood on a patio chair to hang the trap back on its hook.

Do you think there were wasps in the Garden of Eden?" Jason asked.

His dad shrugged his shoulders and smiled.

Jason followed his dad to some soft grass inside a hedge that separated the garden from the rest of the backyard. They could smell the ripe tomatoes as they knelt down together. Jason pressed his face against his dad's chest and wrapped his arms around his waist. Then they bowed their heads, and Jason began to pray.

Ideas for Parents and Children to Discuss

"As our children grow, they need information taught by parents more directly and plainly about what is and is not appropriate. Parents need to teach children to avoid any pornographic photographs or stories. Children and youth need to know from parents that pornography of any kind is a tool of the devil; and if anyone flirts with it, it has the power to addict, dull, and even destroy the human spirit."
—Elder M. Russell Ballard ("Like a Flame Unquenchable," *Ensign*, May 1999, 86)

WHAT IS MODESTY? WHY IS IT IMPORTANT?

"Modesty is an attitude of humility and decency in dress, grooming, language, and behavior. If you are modest, you do not draw undue attention to yourself. Instead, you seek to 'glorify God in your body, and in your spirit' (1 Corinthians 6:20; see also verse 19).

"If you are unsure about whether your dress or grooming is modest, ask yourself, 'Would I feel comfortable with my appearance if I were in the Lord's presence?'"
—*True to the Faith* (Salt Lake City: The Church of Jesus Christ of Latter-day Saints, 2004), 106

"Modesty in dress and manner will assist in protecting against temptation. . . . I do not hesitate to say that you can be attractive without being immodest. You can be refreshing and buoyant and beautiful in your dress and in your behavior."

—President Gordon B. Hinckley ("Stay on the High Road," *Ensign*, May 2004, 114)

"Choose your clothing the way you would choose your friends—in both cases choose that which improves you and would give you confidence standing in the presence of God. Good friends would never embarrass you, demean you, or exploit you. Neither should your clothing."

—Elder Jeffrey R. Holland ("To Young Women," *Ensign*, Nov. 2005, 29)

"Modesty is more than a matter of avoiding revealing attire. It describes not only the altitude of hemlines and necklines but the attitude of our hearts. The word *modesty* means 'measured.' It is related to *moderate*. It implies 'decency, and propriety . . . in thought, language, dress, and behavior' (in Daniel H. Ludlow, ed., *Encyclopedia of Mormonism*, 5 vols. [1992], 2:932)."

—Sister Susan W. Tanner ("The Sanctity of the Body," *Ensign*, Nov. 2005, 14)

WHAT IS PORNOGRAPHY? WHY IS IT EVIL?

"It is like a raging storm, destroying individuals and families, utterly ruining what was once wholesome and beautiful. I speak of pornography in all of its manifestations. . . .

"Suppose a storm is raging and the winds howl and the snow swirls about you. You find yourself unable to stop it. But you can dress properly and seek shelter, and the storm will have no effect upon you.

"Likewise, even though the Internet is saturated with sleazy material, you do not have to watch it. You can retreat to the shelter of the gospel and its teaching of cleanliness and virtue and purity of life."

—President Gordon B. Hinckley ("A Tragic Evil among Us," *Ensign*, Nov. 2004, 59, 61)

"When I consider the demons who are twins—even **immodesty** and **immorality**—I should make them triplets and include **pornography**. They all three go together.

"In the interpretation of Lehi's dream, we find a rather apt description of the destructiveness of pornography: 'And the mists of darkness are the temptations of the devil, which blindeth the eyes, and hardeneth the hearts of the children of men, and leadeth them away into broad roads, that they perish and are lost' [1 Nephi 12:17].

"A modern-day Apostle, Hugh B. Brown, has declared, 'Any immodesty inducing impure thoughts is a desecration of the body—that temple in which the Holy Spirit may dwell' [*The Abundant Life* (1965), 65]."

—President Thomas S. Monson ("Peace, Be Still," *Ensign,* Nov. 2002, 54)

"Choosing to look at images which incite lust will cause the Spirit to withdraw. You have been warned . . . about the dangers of the Internet and the media in putting pornographic images before us. But immodesty is now so common that everyday life requires discipline—a conscious choice not to linger watching whatever might create in us feelings which would repel the Spirit."

—President Henry B. Eyring ("God Helps the Faithful Priesthood Holder," *Ensign,* Nov. 2007, 58)

"Pornography in all its forms is especially dangerous and addictive. What may begin as a curious indulgence can become a destructive habit that takes control of your life. It can lead you to sexual transgression and even criminal behavior. Pornography is a poison that weakens your self-control, changes the way you see others, causes you to lose the guidance of the Spirit, and can even affect your ability to have a normal relationship with your future spouse. If you encounter pornography, turn away from it immediately."

—*For the Strength of Youth* (Salt Lake City: The Church of Jesus Christ of Latter-day Saints, 2001), 17–19

HOW ARE OUR BODIES LIKE TEMPLES?
WHY ARE THEY PRECIOUS?

"Know ye not that ye are the temple of God, and that the Spirit of God dwelleth in you? If any man defile the temple of God, him shall God destroy; for the temple of God is holy, which temple ye are."

—1 Corinthians 3:16–17

"Our physical bodies indeed are temples of God. . . . You and I must carefully consider what we take **into** our temple, what we put **on** our temple, what we do **to** our temple, and what we do **with** our temple. . . .

"Just as the Church's temples portray light and an inner beauty through their outward appearance, so we must be thoughtful and careful about how we dress."

—Elder David A. Bednar ("Ye Are the Temple of God," Rexburg, Idaho, 11 Jan. 2000; available at byui.edu)

"Your body is God's sacred creation. Respect it as a gift from God, and do not defile it in any way. Through your dress and appearance, you can show the Lord that you know how precious your body is. You can show that you are a disciple of Jesus Christ."

—*For the Strength of Youth* (Salt Lake City: The Church of Jesus Christ of Latter-day Saints, 2001), 14

"We came to this earth that we might have a body and present it pure before God in the celestial kingdom. The great principle of happiness consists in having a body. The devil has no body, and herein is his punishment. . . .

"All beings who have bodies have power over those who have not. The devil has no power over us only as we permit him."

—Joseph Smith, *Teachings of the Prophet Joseph Smith* (Salt Lake City: Deseret Book, 1976), 181